ANGRY ALAN

two plays by Penelope Skinner

Fucked

ANGRY ALAN premiered at Underbelly on 2 August 2018 as part of the Edinburgh Fringe Festival, produced by Francesca Moody Productions and Popcorn Group in association with Underbelly and SEARED.

ANGRY ALAN began as a rehearsed reading commissioned by the Aspen Fringe Festival in June 2017.

Cast

Roger	Donald Sage Mackay

Creative Team

Playwright and Director	Penelope Skinner
Producer	Francesca Moody
Lighting	Zak Macro
Sound	Dominic Kennedy
Projection	Stanley Orwin-Fraser
Rehearsals Stage Manager	Anuśka Zaremba-Pike
Associate Producers	SEARED, Charlotte Colbert, Philip Colbert, Jessica Malik
PR	Chloe Nelkin Consulting
Artistic Associate	Maurice LaMee

Supported by DryWrite

FUCKED premiered at the Old Red Lion Theatre on 16 April 2008, produced by Tangram Theatre Company.

Cast

F	Becci Gemmell

Creative Team

Director	Daniel Goldman
Producer	Tangram Theatre Company
Set and Props	Emma Pile
Sound Design	Daniel Goldman and Penelope Skinner
Stage Manager	Keiko LeMon
Casting	Kate Penning

ANGRY ALAN

Donald Sage Mackay Roger

Theatre credits include: *White Guy On The Bus* (Finborough Theatre); *A Moon for the Misbegotten* (Lyric Theatre, Belfast); *Linda* (Manhattan Theatre Club, Off-Broadway); *Fred's Diner* (Magic Theatre); *Our Town* (Actors Theatre of Louisville); *stop. reset.* (Signature Theatre, Off-Broadway); *Blood and Gifts* (La Jolla Playhouse); *His Girl Friday* (La Jolla Playhouse) and *Six Degrees of Separation* (Old Globe Theatre).

Television/Film credits include: *Deep State* (recurring opposite Mark Strong), *The Looming Tower*, *Modern Family*, *Mad Men*, *Masters of Sex*, *Elementary*, *Blue Bloods*, *The Good Wife*, *House*, *The West Wing*, *NCIS*, *Law and Order: SVU*, *Criminal Minds*, *The Shield*, *Frasier*, *Star Trek Enterprise*, *According to Jim*, *ER*, recurring roles on *Scrubs*, *The Practice*, *Providence* and *Transformers: Revenge of the Fallen*.

Donald received an MFA in Acting from the University of California, San Diego and studied at the Moscow Art Theatre.

Penelope Skinner Playwright and Director

Penelope Skinner is a UK-based playwright. Her other new play *Meek* is also premiering at this year's festival at the Traverse Theatre, produced by Headlong.

Other plays include: *Linda* (Royal Court; Manhattan Theatre Club); *The Ruins of Civilization* (Manhattan Theatre Club). *Fred's Diner* (Chichester Festival Theatre; Magic Theatre, San Francisco); *The Village Bike* (Royal Court; MCC); *The Sound of Heavy Rain* (Paines Plough Roundabout Tour); *Eigengrau* (Bush Theatre) and *Fucked* (Old Red Lion; Assembly Rooms, Edinburgh).

She also writes for television and film, and co-wrote a graphic novel *Briony Hatch* with her sister Ginny Skinner. Penelope is also the recipient of the George Devine Award and The Evening Standard Award for Most Promising New Playwright.

Zak Macro Lighting

Zak Macro is a lighting designer based in London. Having studied Lighting Design at The Royal Central School of Speech and Drama, Zak now works as a freelance designer and and re-lighter for many venues and companies both nationally and internationally.

Recent credits include: Lighting Design for *NOISE* (The Old Rep); *White Guy on the Bus* (Finborough Theatre); *Fenech-Soler* (OSLO Hackney); *The Weather Man* (Basic Space Festival); *We Can Make You Happy* (The Vaults); *Jenufa* (The ENO at Lilian Baylis); *Tomorrow* (Above the Arts Theatre) and *Death of a Hunter* (Finborough Theatre).

Other credits include: Re-lighter and Technical Manager for *Chotto Desh* (Akram Khan and Sue Buckmaster World Tour) and Re-Lighter for *Until The Lions* (Akram Khan Company World Tour).

Dominic Kennedy Sound

Dominic Kennedy is a Sound Designer and Music Producer for performance and live events, he has a keen interest in developing new work and implementing sound and music at an early stage in a creative process. Dominic is a graduate from Royal Central School of Speech and Drama where he developed specialist skills in collaborative and devised theatre making, music composition and installation practices. His work often fuses found sound, field recordings, music composition and synthesis.

Recent design credits include: Roundabout Season 2018 (Paines Plough); *The Assassination of Katie Hopkins* (Theatr Clywd); *Ramona Tells Jim* (Bush Theatre); *And the Rest of Me Floats* (Outbox); *I Am a Tree (Jamie* Wood); *Box Clever* (nabokov); *Skate Hard Turn Left* (Battersea Arts Centre); Roundabout Season 2017 (Paines Plough); *Gap in the Light* (Engineer); *Broken Biscuits* (Paines Plough); Roundabout Season 2016 (Paines Plough); *With a Little Bit of Luck* (Paines Plough); *The Human Ear* (Paines Plough); *The Devil Speaks True* (Goat and Monkey); *Run* (Engineer) and *O No!* (Jamie Wood).

Stanley Orwin-Fraser Projection

Stanley graduated from the University of Leeds with BA Honours Degree in Cinema & Photography in 2013.

Stanley's credits include: *Kashchei the Immortal, La Princesse Jaune, Giovanna d'Arco, Macbeth* and *Alzira* (Buxton Opera House); *Privacy,* City of Angels and *One Night In Miami* (Donmar Warehouse); *Still Game: Live, Gary Tank Commander: Live* and *Still Game 2* (SSE Glasgow Hydro); *Idylls of the King* and *Alice in Wonderland* (Oxford Playhouse); *BFG, Singing' in the Rain* and *Ashes* (Bolton Octagon); *Secret Cinema: Star Wars* and *Secret Cinema: 28 Days Later* (Secret Cinema); *Ages* and *Rise* (Old Vic: New Voices); *John Bishop: Supersonic, Dan and Phil: The Amazing Tour Is Not On Fire, Harry and Paul: Legends The Red Shoes, Reasons to Be Cheerful* and *Nativity: The Musical, Up n Under* (Touring); *Stack* and *Goodbear* (Bedlam); *Ghost: The Musical* (English Theatre); *Mother Goose* (Chipping Norton Theatre); *Impossible* (Noel Coward Theatre); *Bodyguard: Das Musical* (Musical Dome Köln); *Deathtrap* (Salisbury Playhouse); *La Boheme* (Hanoi Opera House); *Eurobeat* (Pleasance Grand); *Privacy 2.0* (The Public Theatre); *Cinderella* (London Palladium); *Speech and Debate* (Trafalgar Studios); *Project Polunin* (Sadler's Wells); *Gianni Schicchi* (Nanjing Opera House) *The Christmasaurus* (Hammersmith Apollo); *Strangers on a Train* (Theatre Royal Brighton); *Holes* (Nottingham Playhouse); *The Phlebotomist* (Hampstead Theatre) and *Starlight Express* (Starlight Express Theatre).

Francesca Moody Productions

Francesca has produced theatre in London, Edinburgh, on tour in the UK and internationally. She is the original producer of the multi-award winning and Olivier nominated *Fleabag* by Phoebe Waller-Bridge, which she has presented in Edinburgh, at Soho Theatre on UK tours and internationally in South Korea and Australia for DryWrite in co-production with Soho Theatre.

Other freelance credits include: *Spine* (Soho Theatre/UK Tour: Fringe First and Herald Angel); *Gardening: For the Unfulfilled and Alienated* (Undeb/Pleasance: Fringe First); *Home* (SEARED/Arcola); *Where the White Stops* (Antler/Underbelly); *Jekyll & Hyde* (Flipping the Bird/Assembly/Southwark Playhouse); *Mydidae* (DryWrite/Soho Theatre/Trafalgar Studios) and *Brimstone and Treacle* (SEARED/Arcola).

She is the former Producer at Paines Plough and is currently Executive Producer at curious directive.

THANKS

ANGRY ALAN would not have been possible without the generous support, time, work and advice of the following people:

Charlotte Colbert, Philip Colbert, Jessica Malik, Alex Waldmann, James Grieve, Phyllida Lloyd, Phoebe Waller-Bridge, Vicky Jones, Harriet Bolwell, Matthew Littleford, Richard Lakos, Peter Moody, Giles Moody, Genevieve Moody, Gail Carrodus, Thea Behbahani, Marina Dixon, Tara Wilkinson, Michael Windsor-Ungureanu, Janfarie & Andrew Skinner, Ginny Skinner, Chris Campbell.

Popcorn Group

Popcorn Group was founded by artists Charlotte and Philip Colbert. The company works across art, design, film and TV. Developing powerful creative content for a global audience. The company has dynamically married developing powerful creative content with strategic brand partnerships and collaborations. With Philip Colbert's pop world leading to Popcorn Group projects with Chupa Chups, Peanuts, Made.com and Disney.

Charlotte Colbert is a film-maker and multi disciplinary artist, who has created award-winning short films and screenplays as well as moving imagery installations and large-scale public displays. Charlotte wrote and directed the critically acclaimed short film *The Silent Man* starring Simon Amstell and Sophie Kennedy-Clark.

Jessica Malik has recently joined Popcorn Group as a producer and they are currently developing film and TV projects with writers including Gonzalo Maza (writer of the Academy Award winning film *A Fantastic Woman*), Penelope Skinner, Laurence Coriat, Bafta-winning writer Charlie Covell, Mary Harron (*American Psycho*) and Kitty Percy.

SEARED

SEARED is the creation of actor Alex Waldmann (RSC, Globe, National Theatre, Donmar Warehouse, Almeida, Cheek by Jowl). Founded in 2010, SEARED is an independent production company dedicated to the development and facilitation of work that is provocative, politically conscious, and above all, entertaining.

Previous productions include: the premiere of *Years of Sunlight* by Michael McLean (Theatre 503); sell-out revivals of *Home* by David Storey and *Brimstone and Treacle* by Dennis Potter (Arcola Theatre). Edinburgh Fringe Festival productions include: the premieres of *Rose* by Hywel John, *The Ducks* by Michael McLean and *Pedestrian* by Tom Wainwright.

FUCKED

Becci Gemmell F

Theatre credits include: *The Winter's Tale* (Globe); *The Here and This and Now* (Plymouth Drum/Southwark Playhouse); *Noises Off* (Nottingham Playhouse); *Much Ado About Nothing* (Manchester Royal Exchange); *The Comedy of Errors; Taming of the Shrew* (Globe); *Forever House* (Plymouth Drum); *Foxfinder* (Finborough); *Sixty Five Miles* (Paines Plough/Hull Truck); *66 Books* (Bush Theatre); *Eurydice* (ATC/Young Vic); *As You Like It* (Dash Arts); *F*cked* (Tangram Theatre, Old Red Lion/Assembly Rooms); *Is Everyone OK?* (Nabokov); *How to Disappear Completely...* (Southwark Playhouse); *Mad, Funny, Just* (Creased/Old Vic New Voices) and *Air Guitar* (Bristol Old Vic).

Film credits include: *Red Lights*.

Television credits include: *Land Girls, Code of a Killer, Call the Midwife, Hometime, Angel of Death* and *Casualty*.

Daniel Goldman Director

Daniel is a director, translator, dramaturg and playwright.

Directing credits include: *Thebes Land* (OffWestEnd Award Best Production 2016); *You're Not Like the Other Girls Chrissy* (Stage Award for Best Solo 2010 & Olivier Award Nomination 2011); *Team Viking & A Hundred Different Words for Love* with James Rowland (Vault Festival Origins Award 2016 & Best Show Award 2017); *Fucked* by Penelope Skinner and Tangram's *Scientrilogy* with John Hinton (Adelaide Fringe Best Show Award 2016 & OffWestEnd Award for Best Show for Young People 2015).

Daniel is the founding Artistic Director of both Tangram Theatre Company (www.tangramtheatre.co.uk) and CASA Latin American Theatre Festival (www.casafestival.org.uk).

Emma Pile Director

Emma is a designer, draughtsperson and digital artist for theatre, exhibitions and events. Emma studied Design for Stage at The Royal Central School of Speech and Drama and has since been assisting, drawing and teaching design both in the UK and internationally.

emmapile.net

Tangram Theatre Company

Tangram Theatre Company was founded by Daniel Goldman in London in 2006 to create life-affirming, socially engaged theatre that actively engages its audience. Orignally, comprised of company members Daniel Goldman, Johan Westergren, John Hinton, Omar Elerian and Sibusiso Khambule, Tangram has worked over a hundred artists over the past 12 years to preform 15 critically acclaimed award winning shows to 80,000+ audience members all over the world.

Shows include: *4.48 Psychosis* (Old Red Lion); *Crunch!* (UK & International Tour); *Richard III* (Southwark Playhouse); *Fucked* (Old Red Lion & Assembly Rooms); *The Origin of Species.../ Albert Einstein Relativitively Speaking/The Element in the Room* (UK and International Tour); *Fuente Ovejuna/The Dragon* (Southwark Playhouse) and *Team Viking/A Hundred Different Words for Love/Revelations* (Summerhall & UK Tour).

ANGRY ALAN
&
FUCKED

Two Plays by Penelope Skinner

OBERON BOOKS
LONDON

WWW.OBERONBOOKS.COM

First published in 2018 by Oberon Books Ltd
521 Caledonian Road, London N7 9RH
Tel: +44 (0) 20 7607 3637 / Fax: +44 (0) 20 7607 3629
e-mail: info@oberonbooks.com

A catalogue record for this book is available from the British
Library.

PB ISBN: 9781786826176
E ISBN: 9781786826183

Cover image: The Other Richard

eBook conversion by Lapiz Digital Services, India.

Visit www.oberonbooks.com to read more about all our books and to buy them. You
will also find features, author interviews and news of any author events, and you can
sign up for e-newsletters so that you're always first to hear about our new releases.

www.bloomsbury.com

Contents

ANGRY ALAN

For Donald

Acknowledgements

Donald Sage Mackay. David Ledingham at Aspen Fringe Festival. Hemant Bharatram and Rukmini Chatterjee at the Shriram Centre, Delhi. Francesca Moody. Janfarie & Andrew Skinner. Ginny Skinner. Cathy King at 42. James Grieve at Paines Plough. George Spender and Konstantinos Vasdekis at Oberon Books. The actor Chris Campbell.

I.

Where It All Begins...

ROGER talks to the audience.

Do you ever do that thing where you think to yourself
I should really go for a run
so you look out the window
but hmm. That sky looks kind of *ominous*. Doesn't it?
So you pick up your phone to check the weather
see if it's going to rain
but when you look at your phone you've got a
message or an email so you open the message or the email and
it contains like
a link to an article or whatever so you click on it and
you read it and it's interesting enough to keep you reading to
the end so you read to the end and then at the bottom of the
page you see another link and this one is like
'You're not gonna *believe* what they found when
they cut open this giant snake,' and you're like well okay *that*
I've gotta read so you read it and then next to *that* article is a
photograph of a celebrity on the beach that you need to take a
closer look at so you do and so on and so on and eventually
you realize time has sort of
and it's forty minutes later and you put your phone
down and wonder what you were doing and remember you
were going to go for a run but when you look outside it's
raining so
why am I telling you that? Oh right. Because that is
exactly how I first find Alan. Which when I think about it
is where it all begins. It's Monday morning and just
to provide you with some context
on this particular Monday morning
things are what I would consider to be
normal. Not the old normal. The old normal is long
gone. On a Monday morning

9

Roger-from-before would be getting in his fancy car and heading into the office. But what you're looking at here is Roger-Now. And Roger-Now is the third assistant store manager in the Walnut Creek Safeway and he doesn't work Mondays and if you're wondering what the third assistant store manager does

you know when you have to bring something back to the store and you're complaining to the checker? And she's not dealing with your complaint to your satisfaction so you say,

'I'd like to see the manager'? The guy who comes along at that point? It's not the actual store manager just so you know. His name is Tim and he's sitting up in his fancy glass office on the second floor. We actually went to high school together which is how I got this job. But that's a whole nother story. Point is you don't need to worry about Tim because you never meet Tim. See? But me? Sure. I'm the guy who comes to help. I'm not in a suit I'm in a shirt and tie and I've got a badge and it says my name is Roger and I'm happy to help. And apparently it also says: I'm a guy you can yell at. Sometimes if you're mad enough you can threaten me with physical violence. But I'll just offer you a refund and tell you I'm very sorry and I hope you'll continue to choose Safeway for all your shopping needs. Because that's store policy and I know better than to go up against store policy. Where am I going with this? Oh right. I'm at the beginning. And it's Monday morning

and I'm awake early and I'm considering exercising when I fall into your average google vortex but this time

instead of forty minutes of pointless surfing

I end up watching a video about history

which is kind of amazing

so I watch it again. Then I click on a link underneath to the man who uploaded it. He calls himself Angry Alan. And he's a pioneer of something they call The Men's Rights Movement. Have you heard of that? Apparently what it is is it's a natural evolution from the women's movement because basically:

in a nutshell: since feminism was so successful

things have gone too far the other way. We're now
living in a 'Gynocentric Society' and now
        now it's like Beyonce says: Who runs the world?
Women. And because of this
        ordinary men are really beginning to suffer. And
Alan doesn't just say these things: he backs it up with
evidence. Statistics. Data. He's got his own website. Angry
Alan dot com. He's got his own YouTube Channel. Angry
Alan TV. And before I know it I'm reading more and more
        I spend five hours reading
        and watching videos about men's rights and at certain
points I'm vaguely aware of Courtney coming in going 'What
are you doing?' and I'm like
        'Reading,' and she's like 'What are you reading?' and
I keep reading and she's like 'What are you reading?' and I
keep reading and she says, 'You know Roger
        your ability to ignore the sound of my voice is so
offensively patriarchal,' and I keep reading and she's like
'ROGER,' and I'm like 'What?' and she's like 'Jesus Christ.
Never mind. I'm making a sandwich then I'm going to
Melissa's,' and I'm like
        'Okay sure I'll take a sandwich. Thanks,' and I keep
on reading and watching videos and at some point
        I'm not sure exactly when but at a certain point I find
myself
        up on my feet
        in the bedroom
        and something incredible happens and the best way I
can describe it is like this:

A red light flashes and an alarm sounds. ROGER is in a state of
rapture.

        This is what they call: my red pill moment!

The light/alarm stops.

Because for the first time in a really long time I
feel like someone is speaking to me in a language which I
completely understand and for the first time in a really
really long time I feel like someone is saying
something which makes me feel
like
good about myself. Because you know
I haven't felt good for a while. And I mean maybe
years. And I can say that now. Because one of the first things
Alan talks about is that in our society
men aren't allowed to talk about their feelings. It's so
hard for us men to say things like: Hey. I'm Roger. I feel like I
could have done so much more with my life. I feel inadequate.
I feel like a failure. And until this morning
I didn't even know that's what I was feeling. I thought
maybe I had bowel cancer? Because I've also been reading a
lot of medical websites? And I had a lot of the symptoms. Of a
lot of different diseases. Most of em. Actually. But now I realize
this pain in my gut and the fatigue and the rage I sometimes feel
is the result of the toxicity of my own history and the bearing of
the burden of my own suffering for all these years without ever
acknowledging its legitimacy or even worse
blaming myself for it. But in this moment
here in my bedroom on a Monday morning in May
with the sound of the rain on the window I start to learn
thanks to Alan
that maybe it's not actually all my fault. It's like
it's like
I've been living in a cage, right? I'm like a man who's
been living in a cage but he didn't know it. He was unhappy.
And the reason he was unhappy was because of the cage.
But he didn't know about the cage. So he didn't know why
he was unhappy. And when I take the red pill it doesn't solve
the problem. I'm still in the cage. But at least I *know* about the
cage. And *realizing* that I'm in a cage. Is like

so liberating
that I make a decision: I say to myself these exact
words: out loud I say:
'Things are going to change around here.'
And once I've said it
there's no going back.

MEN'S RIGHTS VIDEO
(about how men are intrinsically GOOD)

I text the video link to Joe. My son?

Me

www.angryalan.com/aremengreatorgood.av

He lives with my ex-wife. And I haven't seen him
for about eight months or something because he's supposedly
having this 'rough time' but no one will tell me what it's
about? So I text him the link. I want to make sure
whatever he's going through
I just want him to know: you're intrinsically good,
son. *We're* good and we're brave and we're clever and people
just like us have done some pretty awesome things and don't
you ever let anyone make you feel like you're not worth
something just because you're a *man*. Of course I don't say
that in my text I just send him the link. But I think he'll get
the message.

II.

fish tacos

So the next significant event

is probably this evening a few weeks later when Courtney
makes fish tacos. Not because of the tacos themselves which are

like much of Courtney's cooking

fairly unremarkable

but because this is when I first find out about the
conference. I've signed up to a couple of men's rights mailing lists
and as a result I've been getting a lot of emails. In fact I haven't
had so many emails since I was at A T&T. And it's keeping me
quite busy. Which is why I'm on my phone during dinner

and I'm just about to open my last unread email

when Courtney takes a big bite of taco

and turns to me and says, 'Are you fucking someone else?'

Courtney can be quite crude by the way so I
apologize but this is what she does she takes a big bite of taco
and then turns to me and says: 'Are you fucking someone
else?' And I say, 'What?' And she says,

and it's quite hard to understand because her mouth
is full plus I'm distracted by the large smear of guacamole on
her cheek but I'm pretty sure she says:

'When Georgette Peterson's husband Arnie started
sleeping with that skinny girl from the thrift store she said one
of the first signs was how much time he suddenly spent on his
cellphone. So I'm asking you Roger: are you fucking someone
else?' and I laugh

because

well first of all because I quite like the idea that I
could be fucking someone else

and I don't immediately want to rule it out as an
imaginary possibility

but also because I'm relieved that I'm not fucking
someone else but instead not only have an innocent explanation
for the amount of time I've been spending on my phone

but also a reason of such immense political importance
and value. And I say, 'No Courtney I'm not fucking someone else
I'm changing the world.' And she says, 'You are?'

And so I explain to her about Alan. They don't teach
Men's Rights at the Community College by the way which
is why Courtney's not aware of the movement. She actually
only discovered feminism last year when she signed up for
her Women's Studies Course. And it's been very inspiring for
her. But I also think it's a big part of why Alan has been such a
breath of fresh air for me. I kind of knew

this whole time

that there was something not quite right about the
things she's been coming out with? Like all these factoids
about how bad things 'still are' for women? Alan debunks
a lot of them on his website. So I run through the basics for
Courtney. I teach her about gynocentric sexism. About how
men are raised to value women's feelings over our own. How
we're taught early on that our only worth as human beings
lies in being financial providers. And I'm just explaining how
women have been exploiting this for years when Courtney
starts smiling. And I say, 'Is something funny?' And she
goes 'What's this about, Roger? Is this about me going to the
Community College?' and I say, 'No. What? What are you
talking about? And she says, 'Okay then,' and she gets up
and starts clearing the plates and I'm like 'Are you not even
the slightest bit interested?' And she says, 'Nope. Not really.
Sounds kinda dumb,' and off she goes into the kitchen. Starts
washing up already. So

I'm left here feeling pretty offended and thinking
how nice it must be to feel so blasé about the oppression of
approximately half the human race and I decide

before I go help with the dishes

just to check that last unread email:

From: MRKentucky@aool.com
To: RogerMcCleod64@qwickmail.net
Subject: Cincinnati Conference on Men's Rights

Tickets now on sale for this event on August
16th and 17th

and turns out Alan is organizing a men's rights
weekend conference in Cincinnati. And I think: how cool
would that be? To be surrounded by people who understand
why and how much this stuff matters?! And look! Alan himself
is giving the keynote speech! Can you imagine? To hear
Alan talk in person? I think that would be something quite
inspirational! But then I look at the price of the tickets and
I think: whoah

okay well. Maybe not. Maybe next time.

III.

a son!

A photograph of Joe

This is Joe. People say he looks like me. What do you think? He's such a great kid. He's into arts and acting but he's not one of those nerds who gets picked last for the sports team. He's outdoorsy too. You know? Like I was. And it's funny because when I get his text

I'm just about to head into work and I get his text and it stops me in my tracks. I'm out here on the driveway

about to get in my car and I read his message and suddenly I get this vivid memory of me and Suzanne

when Suzanne was pregnant

going to that scan where they tell you what kind of baby you're having? And I remember when the nurse lady first said it's a boy

and I looked at Suzanne and I said 'It's a boy!' and she said it's a boy! and it was like in that split second this whole future just unrolled in my imagination

how we'd hang out together. Just me and him. Go hiking and hunting and camp out in the wilderness. How I'd teach him all the stuff my dad taught me. How to whittle a stick to catch a fish. And use a gun. And build a fire. A son I thought. A son! And then he's born and it's like

crazy and we don't sleep and Suzanne gets post-natal depression which I don't know if anyone here has ever experienced that but it was extremely challenging for me? And next thing I know we're getting divorced and then I lose my job and I move away and I'm paying all this alimony but I don't see Joe except on weekends or holidays. And the older he gets the more of a stranger he seems to become and then he stops visiting altogether and no one will tell me why so of course I blame myself? Right? But then I take the red pill.

And I learn about how the entire legal system and the structure of the family courts are rigged

to favor women. And mothers. And meanwhile men like me

fathers who love their kids

are getting exploited. Suzanne got custody. I've paid her all this alimony. Over many years. And in return I've been alienated from Joe through absolutely no fault of my own. And I find myself standing in the driveway about to get in my car reading a text from my son

Me
www.angryalan.com

Joe
LOL.
Can we meet up? Need to talk to you.

saying he loves me
sorry I just
saying that he loves me a lot

and that he wants to see me because there's something he needs to talk to me about. And I just feel so elated. Because at last

he's going to confide in me about this 'rough time' he's been having. And I'm going to get a chance to help him finally. And all it took was for me to stop blaming myself

and to reach out to him with a profoundly important message about his self-worth

and at last we've got a chance to build a real relationship. So.

Beat.

Now we've just got to find a time to actually meet. We're going back and forth with dates at the moment. Modern age eh? Kid's fourteen. He's got to 'find time in his calendar'.

MEN'S RIGHTS VIDEO
(about the male gaze)

IV.

#metoo

So it's a Thursday night and it's nice weather and
me and Courtney are out for a pizza with some friends of hers
from work
Nadine and Melissa
nice girls
and since the tacos things have been a bit tense
between me and Courtney? Not terrible. But she keeps making
little comments like 'Can you pass the salt Roger or does that
violate your human rights?' or 'Oh hey Roger. Here in the
Matrix the trash cans need to go out'. So you know. Suffice to
say my attempts to convert her have so far been unsuccessful
and we're sitting in the booth in the corner and we
order some drinks and we're deciding what to eat and they're
all secretaries at the same law firm
and they're going on about work so I'm half looking
at the menu but also checking my emails when I hear
Courtney say, 'Well we've got to do something. We can't just
let him get away with it,' so I listen in
and turns out they're discussing some guy at work
who they're planning to hashtag metoo? His name is Paul
and he's apparently been 'harassing' Nadine for months
and I'm looking at Nadine and I'm remembering the
video I watched this morning and let's just say Nadine has a
lot of gaze-harvesting techniques going on
so I say, 'Now hold your horses girls
how do you know he's harassing you?'
and they tell me Paul keeps asking Nadine out.
Wanting to see her outside the office. And I say, 'Well. Okay.
Maybe he likes you. You're a single lady. Isn't it possible
he thinks he's being romantic?' And Courtney says: 'He's
her boss, Roger'. And Melissa says: 'Is it romantic to email
her pornography?' And Nadine says: 'Is it romantic to tell
everyone at work that he had sex with me when it's not true?'

And I say, 'Okay. But. Could he have had a good reason?'
which is when Courtney leans over the table and hisses
    'Roger? Be quiet please. You are *embarrassing* me!'
which once upon a time might have worked on me but I'm sorry
    I said things are gonna change around here. And
that means when the situation calls for someone to speak out
against the oppressive Gynocratic Regime? I can no longer
remain silent. So I say, 'Look. The truth is
    according to my friend Alan
    these witch hunts
    that have happened as a result of this hashtag metoo
    are extremely detrimental to our justice system.
Does a man not even get the right to a fair trial? What
happened to innocent until proven guilty?' And Nadine's like
'Paul's not being put on trial, Roger. I was just going to tweet
about it'. And I say, 'Okay well then but it's trial by media.'
And Melissa says, 'Are you telling us you don't agree with
hashtag metoo?' And I say, 'What I'm telling you Melissa is
that you women need to think about what it is you actually
want. Because Alan says Modern American Woman wants it
all her own way: she wants her own career. *And* she wants a
rich guy to treat her like a princess. She wants you to respect
her intellectually. *Then* she invites her girlfriends over to watch
Fifty Shades of Grey. She wants to be president. *And* she wants to
be spanked on
the bottom in the bedroom. And you can't have both now.
Can you? Because meanwhile'
    I say
    and I'm on a roll now I say,
    'Alan says Modern American Men are getting more
and more confused. And we're taking more and more of the
blame when you women don't get what you want.'
    Which is when Courtney kicks me under the table
    she actually kicks me in the shins and she says, 'You
know what I want Roger? I want you to shut your face!'

    Beat.

In her defense

Courtney's very sensitive about anything to do with
'harassment' because of what happened to her mom. But you
know the other way round? Like if I kicked Courtney

in a restaurant

in front of our friends?

you'd call that abusive. So

V.

impulse buy

I wait for her to be asleep and I go online

and Christ knows what she's going to say about me
spending this kind of money but I say the following words out
loud: Fuck Courtney, I say. Not quite that loud because she's
only in the next room, I say it more like: *Fuck Courtney.* And I
go onto Angry Alan dot com and I click

and I click

and I pay

and I'm going to the conference in Cincinnati and
I'm feeling pretty excited about it when the page comes up
you know the page saying the payment's gone through

and thank you for your payment

except now it's offering me the chance to donate.
The suggested amount is a hundred dollars.

DONATE

**you can make a donation to support
Alan's charitable work with men and boys**

And suddenly I imagine myself

I imagine Roger

walking into that conference

holding his head up high because he's made a real
contribution. He's helped fund a home for men who are
victims of domestic violence. Or or or survivors of male
genital mutilation. And before I know it I'm logging into my
online banking and checking my account and okay oh dear
that's worse than I thought because my alimony payment has
already come out but no okay it's doable. How about

instead of staying at the conference hotel

I get my tent out of the garage? Book a spot at a
KOA campground outside of Cincinnati. That could save a
bunch of money. And uh okay I can do some overtime next

month and maybe put my stamp collection on eBay which
I've been meaning to do for ages anyway and I go back to the
window I click on the button and I'm doing it
     I'm donating
     what can only be described as a significant financial
contribution to the Men's Rights Movement. And I feel this
kind of
     like an exhilaration. Like I'm changing. You know?
I'm becoming someone new.

VI.

two dozen eggs

Alan points out how unfair it is that in an emergency
like on a sinking ship
the rule is you have to save women and children
first. He says this is because men's lives are considered to
be innately less valuable. Are we men disposable, he asks?
Are we less worthy of saving for some reason? If a ship was
sinking who would you rather save? A stranger or your own
son? Your own father? See when you take the red pill you start
to question all the things you've just taken for granted your
whole life
like how you as a man are meant to be some kind of
a hero
or else there's something wrong with you. And how
one of your jobs
as a man
is to go around saving women from whatever situation
they've gotten themselves into
while you yourself are left drowning. This is what I'm
thinking about as I'm supervising a spillage in Aisle 7. And
then Charlene comes over and asks me to go to Register 3
because the new bagger is in trouble again. So I head over and
when I get here
I see the bagger Martin looking all sheepish and his
hands are covered in egg yolk and there's a woman here
a woman who is let's just say quite an unattractive woman
probably menopausal
and she's standing here
holding a carton of eggs to her chest like it's a wounded
animal or something
and weeping
and I remember what Alan says in his video on male
suicide: about how seventy percent of the people who kill
themselves in America are men

because we're raised not to show our feelings. See?
All we hear about all the time is how much women suffer
and meanwhile guys like me for example
my wife walks out on me and takes my kid
then I live through 2008
lose everything I've worked twenty years for
and you know what?
I haven't cried in front of another human being since
I was eight years old. So I'm looking at this woman in a new
light, right? I now recognize her tears for what they are: a
weapon of manipulation. And I can hear Alan's voice in my
head and he's saying, 'Roger. Don't be a White Knight. She
doesn't care about those eggs. She just wants money off. Same
as they all do.' But what can I do? New Roger wants to speak
up. He wants to call her out on her mercenary BS. But Store
Policy dictates the customer's always right so I say, 'Ma'am let
me get you a refund on those eggs,' and I go get her two more
cartons and I pack them myself. And she goes away happy.
Course she does. But next thing you know Martin the new
bagger is being called up to Tim's office and turns out this is
his third strike
and he's gone. Just like that. An honest man loses his job
because a woman wanted free eggs! I'm sorry I'm just
it's just so unfair and I just

Beat.

I end up back here on my own
hiding behind a big palette of cereal boxes and
feeling kinda
I don't know. Because it takes me right back to AT&T
and that day in Bill Jefferson's office when he told me they
were letting me go. The look on his face. This look like
sorry man. It's just one of those things.
I should just go get my gun I thought. Because there's
not much use for me now. A middle-aged guy starting all over
again in this market? People want twenty-three year olds fresh
out of college or even eighteen year olds who were smart

enough not to go! But guys like me? Twenty years' experience at a company like A T&T means diddly squat apparently

I mean thank goodness for me I met Courtney when I did. Otherwise

yeah

ROGER mimes shooting himself in the head.

So of course I want to do something to get justice for Martin. I'll go into Tim's office I think. Threaten to quit. 'If he goes I go.' Right? Right! Let's go see Tim! But then I remember the money I spent on the conference and the donation and the kind of financial position I'd be in if I didn't have this job and I think okay well listen

I'm going to the conference. And I'm supporting men's charities. So when you think about it maybe I'm already doing enough for men like Martin. And maybe this is a case of pick your battles. So. Okay. So for now. I'll stay quiet.

Messages ping from Joe. Hey Dad, can you send me your dates?/ Can do any weekend in July./ You got any dates in August? /Dad call me about dates. /I can't do 21st anymore can do 16th. Can you let me know? /Dad?

VII.

crazy woman

I mean if I was a person inclined toward this kind of thinking then at this point I'd wonder if there is a conspiracy to stop me going to the conference. First of all

despite having a 'rough time'

Joe appears to have the social life of the Great Gatsby and the weekend of the conference is now the only weekend in the entire summer break when he's free to visit

and secondly this evening

about two weeks before the conference

when I finally get around to telling her I'm going

me and Courtney reach crisis point. And it's very interesting because just before me and Courtney have the argument we're about to have

I listened to Alan's podcast on the warning signs of 'borderline personality disorder' because as it turns out crazy women are a real problem in our society

and the woman you're in a relationship with can be the most dangerous. No offence to any of the ladies present. But guys? We need to be on our guard. See? So anyway. Here we are we're about to eat. And Courtney's made a potato salad and we're at the dining room table

and I tell her I'm planning to go to the conference

and that she might be interested to know the schedule actually contains talks by several *women*

and she says, 'Oh god Roger you're not serious,' and I say, 'No you gotta listen because one of these women okay she used to be a feminist just like you and then she learned about Men's Rights and she totally changed her mind and now

she actually speaks out against feminism and she's a highly educated professional journalist writing for (among other things) a real British newspaper called

uh oh wait what was it called

the Daily Mail?' And I say: 'See it's nothing like you said. It's not just a bunch of angry middle aged white guys flapping around like dying fish out of water because "progress" has made them feel disempowered. Okay? Gasping for air. Okay? No. See? Because there's white *women* too.' And she says, 'They found a couple of idiot women prepared to take their side and now you think I'm going to change my whole opinion?' And I say, 'Not a couple of idiot women. There's a whole organization of em. They call themselves the Honey Badgers. They've got an official website and everything. You want me to send you the link?' Which is when Courtney says:

'Roger?

I think I'm falling out of love with you.'

Beat.

And I say,

'What are you talking about?' And she says: 'If I'm honest Roger? I think you're having some kind of a breakdown. You know? I think you're still very angry about A T&T.' And this Alan guy is feeding that anger. And it's not healthy.' And I say, 'Courtney? You are way off the mark.' And she says, 'So you're not still angry about A T&T?' And I say, 'I didn't say that. Course I'm still angry. I'm saying that's got nothing to do with Alan.' And she says, 'But it was such a long time ago Roger. Are you going to be angry about it the rest of your life?' And I say, 'Well. Unless they apologize. Unless one day Bill Jefferson comes to my front door and says he's sorry for ruining my life. Why Courtney? Are you saying I shouldn't be angry? What are you saying?' And she says, 'I don't know Roger. I guess I just don't look at you that way. And I say, 'What way?' And she says, 'Like a man whose life has been ruined. Because so what if you lost your big shot job? So what if you don't drive a fancy car? So what if you can't go around telling other people what to do? Look at Tim.' And I say, 'What about Tim?' And she says, 'You hate Tim.' And even though I really do hate Tim I say, 'What are you talking about? Tim's my buddy!' And she says, 'I just sometimes think the most powerful men aren't necessarily the nicest men or

the happiest men or the men with the best lives.' And I say,
'I have literally no idea what Tim has to do with this.' And
she says, 'I'm trying to make you feel better, Roger.' And I
say, 'Oh really? By reminding me how powerful and rich Tim
is compared to me? Do you want to fuck Tim? Is that what
you're telling me?' And she says, 'I'm telling you I don't want
you to go to this conference!' and I say, 'Well you know what?
I don't want to hear it.' And I walk away. I walk away. Because
Alan says that's the best thing to do when a woman is being
out of control crazy

   Beat.

      Courtney's insistence on equality doesn't extend to
night-time comforts so

      I'm sleeping on the couch. And I don't know. I guess
until I decide whether I love her enough to sacrifice going to
the conference? Is that

      I mean is that the choice I'm being offered right now?
Courtney or the conference? Joe or the conference? Is that it?
Or is this in fact

      you know is this the moment in the story when the
hero is faced with great adversity? And he has to overcome
these obstacles in order to succeed?

VIII.

the orange lamp

At first there's a certain novelty. The bathroom's always free. I eat nothing but takeout chicken burritos. I drink beer for breakfast. I watch TV naked with my butt on Courtney's special armchair. And every spare minute I'm not at the store

I spend online

reading and watching videos and truthfully? Okay

maybe I get quite into researching the Honey Badgers and where they live and if there are any in my local area. Which there aren't. But there are quite a few going to the conference so I use thinking about that to keep my spirits up. Fantasizing about sitting down to dinner with a woman who doesn't just

argue

about

everything but the fact is

Beat.

truth is the house feels very empty without Courtney.
And it's not like I didn't try

because I did

I tried explaining how important this is for me

I explained why feminism is damaging

I explained how men are suffering

but it didn't do any good. The sad truth is that Courtney is so jaded because of what happened in her own family? In the end she packed a bag

and stood at the end of the bed

and I said 'Please don't go'

and she said: 'You know the first time my stepdad got arrested Roger

I thought we were going to be safe

because he'd go to jail for the rest of his life

and I just feel like if the legal system was as rigged towards women as you keep saying

he would have gone to jail the first time
or the second time
maybe even the third time
but he wouldn't have been free to do what he did and
maybe my mom would still be able to see properly. Roger. Can
you explain that? Can you please explain how the system is so
in favor of women
that my Mom is now partially blind?' And I said 'Courtney
all domestic violence is wrong. Okay? Whether it be
women against men or' – and she said 'How many men die
each week because they are murdered by their spouse Roger?'
And I said 'I don't know Courtney because I don't accept
all those Gynocentric media statistics anymore,' and she said
'I'm leaving you'
and I said 'Okay'
and she said 'Okay'
and I said 'I hope you're taking your orange lamp
because I don't want it cluttering up my hallway!' Which is
mean. Obviously. And I regret it. But
you know
obviously I was upset.

Beat.

The good news is is I can go to the conference now
without anyone giving me grief. And Joe's coming
camping. So
oh right. I didn't say. That was my brilliant idea. So I get
to do both. I bring Joe out to Cincinnati on Saturday night. He
can stay in the tent with me. I still get to go to the whole first day
of the conference then on Sunday morning we can go for a hike
maybe do a little shooting or fishing
he can tell me whatever this big thing is he needs to
talk to me about
and we can get back to the hotel in time for Alan's
keynote speech. Pretty inspiring for Joe don't you think?
To hear Alan speak in person. I wish I'd had that kind of
opportunity when I was fourteen that's for damn sure.

IX.

cincinnati

So I get here on the Friday night
pitch my tent at the KOA
and it's okay, the campsite's kinda gross and it's near
the shore of this big man-made lake so it's pretty humid but
it's fine. And I sleep okay although I'm extremely nervous and
I wake up at dawn and I get to the hotel bright and early.
I'm still anxious because I don't know anyone but I come
into the conference room and it's very nice
nice big windows and all the chairs laid out and a
little stage with a podium and a screen
very professional very organized looking
and there's a table with sticky name labels and I get
a very pleasant surprise to discover that my sticky name label
has a gold rim
and the gold rim apparently means that I'm a donor.
Isn't that something? So I stick it on
feeling pretty good about myself

ROGER is now wearing a name badge with a gold rim.

and I grab a bottle of water and I hang around on my
own for a while trying not to look awkward
and as the room gets more crowded people start
mingling and I get talking to a couple of guys and they're
real friendly. And the whole scene is very upbeat and quite
exciting and I start to feel somewhat like my old self again,
you know? It's kinda like when I used to go to conferences
back in the day with A T&T. Little coffee cups all laid out on
a table and the sound of men laughing and talking and we're
all here for a common purpose. And because of that purpose
we matter. You know? I meet Jamie from California who's a
building contractor. And I meet Dave from Aspen who's also
got a gold name badge. And they're both divorced like me
and we talk about how we ended up here and then something

very exciting happens which is I see Alan for the first time.
Across the room. He just walks in like any other guy. Maybe
he's a little smaller than I thought? But there he is. And I'd
love to go over

>>should I go over?

>>but no he's immediately surrounded by a bunch of
people who all want to talk to him and then the sessions begin
and for a while I forget all about Alan because I have to tell you

>>being here

>>it's not just that it's inspiring

>>it's not just I'm making all these new friends it's like

>>remember that cage I was telling you about? Being
here it's like the bars of that cage are finally lifting. With every
speaker that gets up on that podium I start to feel more and
more optimistic that we could one day live in a world where
all of this injustice that I feel

>>all of this injustice that I know has been affecting me

>>I start to feel like maybe one day we could live in a
world without it

>>because it starts to feel like old times you know?
The jokes people are making

>>some of these jokes I wouldn't repeat but the people
here are just laughing and I mean the women too they're just
laughing and cheering and clapping and one of the speakers

>>he's talking about false rape allegations

>>and he makes one joke

>>it gets a laugh so big they have to turn his mic up
because we're just so pumped with the frikkin freedom of it
all because you don't realize

>>until you get here you don't realize just how oppressive
the Gynocentric Society is. You get used to living your life

>>feeling bad about who you are

>>feeling guilty

>>feeling anxious in case you do or say something
which once upon a time would've been totally fine but in this
day and age is suddenly completely unacceptable for reasons

33

you are unable to comprehend and living your life in terror
that if you put one foot out of line
        you will be viciously and violently attacked on the
internet and feminist lynch mobs will trash your reputation.
And that's no way to live. That's no life at all. Is it?

   Beat.

        I can't wait to meet Alan. I've got it all planned.
I'm going to wait till after his talk tomorrow then I'll go up to
him and shake his hand and say, 'Alan? Thank you
        from the bottom of my heart. Because if it wasn't for
men like you
        men like me and Dave and Jamie
        we'd be on our own in this world. You know?
        Misunderstood.
        And completely frikkin powerless.'

MEN'S RIGHTS VIDEO
(about Trump election)

X.

honey badger

So it gets to evening

amazing day. Best day ever. And my new friends
from the conference head into the bar at the hotel but there's
no way I can afford even one beer at hotel prices so I make
my excuses and head back to the campsite. I've got a couple
of hours to kill before Joe's bus gets in and by now of course
I'm getting nervous about whatever this 'thing' is he needs to
talk to me about. Is he being bullied? Or is it drugs? Or girls?
Or or or or even

you know

is he wondering if he 'likes'

'boys'

not that I'm saying that's what it is but of course it's
crossed my mind as a possibility. I know he's into 'theatre'.
So. And I'm not saying I'd find it easy but I'd be okay with it.
You know?

I'm open minded. I just want to make sure he knows
I'm here for him. So anyway I've cleaned the gun and laid out
the fishing tackle and I'm just rolling out the spare sleeping
bag when I realize it smells musty so I come outside to air it
which is when I see the young blonde woman standing by the
shore of the lake

and it's a warm night and the bugs are out

and I recognize her from the conference and I notice
she's looking kinda glum

and I think Roger? that Honey Badger could be in
trouble! So I go over and I say, 'Hey

you're at the conference right?' And she says, 'Oh
yeah. Hi.' And I say, 'Roger.'

He points at his gold name badge.

And she says, 'Sam.' And I say, 'What a day eh?'
And she says, 'Yeah'. And I say,

because I'm trying to cheer her up I say,

'You know I was so excited when I found out about the Honey Badgers'

and she says, 'I bet'

and I say, 'I just think it's so cool that there are young women out there like you who actually get where we're coming from!' And she says, 'Uh huh.' And I say, 'I'm super excited about tomorrow! Aren't you? I can't wait to hear Angry Alan talk in person. I'm a big fan of his work he's the one who kind of got me into all this so'

and she says, 'Yeah I'm hoping to interview him. He's very controversial isn't he?' And I say, 'Interview?' Which is when she reveals

get this

she's not a Honey Badger

she's a 'vlogger' from some online thing

and she flew here from New York to cover the conference *from a feminist perspective.'*

Can you believe that? Just my luck! They're frikkin everywhere! And I'm like gosh darnit is nothing sacred? Can't we have one weekend to ourselves? I mean I don't say that of course because for a feminist she's surprisingly attractive and I figure there's no harm in just talking for a while so I say, 'Oh how interesting and how are you finding the conference?' and she says, 'Yeah it's fine I just wasn't expecting it to be so hard

to sit in that room and listen to all those comments because,' she says,

'I agree that men have issues and of course you have rights but I just don't understand why you're all so angry with women'. And I say, 'Well women are angry with men, aren't you? Feminists are the angriest women of all. Aren't you a feminist?' And she says, 'Yes.' She says, 'I am. And I'm angry too. But you're looking in the wrong direction. Because if you hate the way society makes you feel then look to the people who actually run society. Look at corporate greed! Look at the one percent! Because you can blame Donald Trump's mother for Donald Trump if you want

but it's not going to change anything.' And before
I've even had a chance to ask what the hell Trump's got to do
with it she points her finger at my chest and she's going 'Oh
and by the way? I see you're one of the poor idiots with a gold
name badge? So just so you know. Because I looked into it.
Alan doesn't give any of your money to charities for men. He
keeps it all. For himself. To fund him sitting on his ass making
angry videos. And he calls it *raising awareness.* So there you go.'
And just like that she walks away.

Beat.

ROGER looks down at his name badge.

I mean

you know

it's not like I believe her. I don't. But even if it's
true? Awareness is ninety percent of the problem and raising
awareness is a huge contribution. So my donation is valid. It's
a completely valid contribution.

I may not have saved any actual lives. Yet. And I'm
sad about my stamp collection. But I've still made a difference.
So. No. There's nothing to feel bad about on my account. You
know? The most important thing is I'm here and I'm having
a great time. And I've got my son coming up to see me. And
we're going to get to know each other again and things are
good you know? Things are really when you think about it
things are just about perfect.

XI.

precipice

A long pause.

I have a son.
That's what I say: I say, 'I have a son. His name is Joe.'

Beat.

I'm sorry I'm all over the place. I've missed a bit.
I need to start before. Before
like when it's morning and we're in the woods early
and it's a beautiful day. I've got the gear in a duffel bag and
the gun on a strap on my shoulder
and Joe's got his little backpack and he's carrying the
lunch and the water
and the birds are singing and we hike for a good
couple of hours and eventually we get to a clearing
and we sit down to drink some water
and I can tell he's about to come out with it
but when he does

Beat.

I say, 'What does your mom say about all this?' and
he says, 'She's getting used to it. Slowly. Why didn't she tell
me?' I say. And he says, 'Because I asked her not to. Because I
wanted to tell you myself. In person. Even though it was really
hard Dad. I've been feeling sick for days. Are you mad at me?'
I say, 'No. I'm mad at your mother. Clearly this is
because of that school she sent you to.' And he says, 'It's got
nothing to do with school, Dad. I've been feeling this way for
ages.' And I say, 'Ages? My god. You haven't even been alive
for *ages* Joseph. What about football? Hockey? What about that
girl from your drama club. Sandra – Sally – whatshername?'
And he says, 'Sara Caruso?' And I say, 'Right. I thought you
had a crush on her?' And he says, 'So?' And I say, 'Well'

38

and he says, 'Dad: I'm not gay. I'm just saying

I don't identify as a male.' And I say, 'I literally don't even know what that means. You got a dick don't you?' And he says, 'So?' And I say, 'So? So! So

you are a male.' And he says, 'It depends on your definition.' And I say, 'No it doesn't. It's a biological reality.' And he says, 'I knew you'd say that. So I bought you a book. Can I read you some?' And he opens up his little pack

and takes out this book he's been carrying and reads me part of it

Both women's and trans liberation have presented me with two important tasks. One: to join the fight to strip away the discriminatory and oppressive values attached to masculinity and femininity. Two: to defend gender freedom – the right of each individual to express their gender in any way they choose, including the right to change their sex, whether female, male, or any point on the spectrum between.

Extract from Leslie Feinberg's *Transgender Warriors*

Do you have any idea what any of that means? Because I sure as hell don't. And I look at him and I go: 'Joe.' And he says, 'Katie.' And I say, 'You have got to be shitting me. I'm sorry but no.' I say, 'I have a son. His name is Joe.' And he doesn't say anything. And I say, 'Is this because me and your mother got divorced?' He says, 'No.' 'Is it because I wasn't around enough?' He says, 'No. Dad.' And I say, 'Then what is it? Is it a phase?' And he says, 'It's not a phase. It's how I feel. And it's what I want.' And I say okay, 'So what does it mean because because because because if you don't believe in gender

if you're telling me you don't believe in gender then,' and he says, 'I believe in gender freedom' and I say, 'Okay but what does that actually mean? In like practical reality are we talking about are we talking about?'

and what I want to say is are we talking about you
wanting to chop your dick off because I swear to god if that's
what he wants I'm going to march him back down to that
campsite and lock him in the car till he comes to his senses but
he seems to know what I'm asking and he goes

'Okay Dad lots of people do and I'm not against it
but I'm not interested in surgical intervention.' And I say, 'You're
not?' And he says, 'No. But I do want to wear dresses and
make up and high heels and I want to challenge the notions of
gender that exist in mainstream society.' And I say, 'Well surely
you can just identify as a girl without wearing a dress son.
I mean Courtney is a girl and she only ever wears jeans and
sneakers unless she's going to a wedding or a funeral,' and he
says, 'Exactly: I just want to be able to choose! Why do we
have to be boxed in by these narrow definitions of what is or is
not a man?' And I say, 'You don't son

but please don't start wearing dresses.' And he says,
'You're ashamed of me.' And I say, 'I just think I should have
been consulted!' And I say, 'Your god damn mother should
have consulted me. Okay? I'm not a nobody in this situation,
Joe. I'm your father!' and he says, 'You always say that word.
Father like it's got some magical power or something. It's just
a gendered word for parent, Dad. You know that, right?' And
I say, 'This is not a game okay, son? This could affect your
whole future. People find out about this? What about when
you want to try and get a job? And he says,

'Please Dad! I need you to accept me! I'm not asking
for permission,' and I say, 'No? Well maybe that's the problem
here. You know? Because who's gonna pay for these dresses
you're going to be wearing? Huh? Who pays for every god
damn thing you own? Huh?
I do! I pay for the clothes on your back and the food on your
table and that means I get to be involved! I have a right to be
involved!' And suddenly as I'm saying this everything starts
crashing in on me in waves: all the injustice. All the things I've
read and seen. How unfair it all is and how helpless I feel and
how angry I am because of all the things I've had taken away
from me – my job

Suzanne

years of alimony

Courtney

my basic human rights

and now my own son? And I can hear Alan's voice
loud in my head saying my God Roger how much more can
you take? how much more of this are you going to take? And
that's when I just let go: I say, 'I am so sick of this shit. Do you
know that? I'm sick of you

disrespecting me

and your mother

scrounging off me

and I'm sick of everyone always

turning everything around and blaming me

and I'm sick of people thinking I'm a piece of shit
they can just walk all over do you hear me? Do you know
what it cost me to raise you? Do you have any idea what I've
sacrificed for your sake? Do you?' And for some reason he's
got his hands up in the air and his eyes are wide and fearful
and I realize as I've been saying all this I realize I've grabbed
the gun somehow

from off my shoulder and somehow I've got the gun
in my hands and I didn't mean to but I'm pointing it at him

I'm standing here

pointing the gun at Joe

and he's staring at me and his eyes are wide with
something like

terror

and I say, 'I'm not gonna

Joe'

but he doesn't say anything he's just standing there
shaking and I say, 'I think I need to take a walk okay?

okay?

I need to take a walk,' and I put the gun down

carefully I place the gun down on the ground

and I back away

and I leave him there

and I go on up the trail through the woods

I walk and I keep walking until I come out of the woods and up past a bullfrog pond and I'm high up into the hills now and I can't walk any more so I stop

on the edge of the rocks

over a wide valley

I can see the lake far below

and there's a buzzard circling in the air

and I stand

looking out over the country

this country

the country where I was born and raised and where I've lived my whole life

and I wonder what's going to become of us. Because this can't be the future can it? Everyone just

changing the rules. Deciding who we are just doesn't

I mean

I can't just decide one day not to be a man, can I?

I'm a man.

I'm a man. And deep down I know that's what my son is too. Course he is. He's a man. He's a man. I'm a man –

The sound of a single gunshot echoes around the valley from far below.

What was that?

Did you hear that?

Sounded like –

Realization of what has happened dawns on ROGER. He stays very still, horrified. He takes a sharp breath. There is the sound of lapping water not far away. ROGER struggles for breath. The faint sound of fish tails slapping on the ground. It goes on for a long time.

The End.

FUCKED

For MB

#metoo

Acknowledgements

Acknowledgements

Daniel Goldman at Tangram Theatre. Becci Gemmell. Matt Morrison. Giles Smart.

A screen is illuminated with a projection.

TODAY.

A projection is added:

Right now.

F reads from a notebook.

The Lion Rampant. By me.

she opens the notebook:

Aged twelve and a half.

Highly emotive medieval music.

Duke Randalf LionArm, the greatest and strongest man in all England, gazed at the beautiful red haired peasant girl who knelt at his feet. "My wife the charitable and good lady Ermeldadrew lies dying of the dreaded plague!" he shouted. "And I can think of nothing in the world except you – you seductive devil!"

He kissed her then, pushing her down onto the hay. For they were in a barn.

"I must have you now," he said.

Isabella closed her eyes and felt her heart swell with love for the noble nobleman. Their passion was as hot as the inner molten core. I will wait for this man, she thought. However long it takes. Ours is a love as true as the earth is flat. And no matter what happens, however hard it will be, I must find a way for us to stay together.

Blackout. A definition is projected onto the wall:

1ST JANUARY

1 Year Ago

Whore

noun.

A prostitute; a harlot.

Another definition is added:

verb.

1.   To have unlawful sexual intercourse; to practice lewdness.

2.   To worship false and impure gods.

A bedroom. F is sitting on the edge of the bed. There is stuff emptied out all over the floor.

A mess. Amongst the mess is the notebook from scene one.

It's not at all uncommon for relationships to end at the new year. Apparently. I read that. Ages ago. And it's funny isn't it because if I didn't already hate new year, if I hadn't always sort of – hated – new year then I probably never would have agreed to work last night do you know what I mean?

Beat.

But they told me – they said it would be a very big night. Big money, they said. People get very drunk on new year's eve, and when people – by people they mean men – when men get very drunk – they spend a lot of money. So goes the theory. Yes? So I was very much expecting to come home from work last night loaded. Needing, actually, to come home loaded because my current financial situation is …well. For example, on my way in to the club last night I was hungry, right, and because I had no cash, the only way I could afford to get anything to eat was with my Boots advantage points. And turns out I only had enough for a Tracker bar so I had to go in Sainsbury's and shoplift a baguette. At that point of course, I still had my travelcard.

Beat.

And I'm saying to myself, right then. Tonight, what we need
is a large and profitable night. No getting drunk and not doing
dances. If we do well tonight we can have a rest later in the
week. I use the we, for some reason, when I talk to myself like
this. Anyway, the early bird, as they say, catches the worm.
So I make sure I get to work early. Straight to the dressing
room. Trowel on the make up. Perfume. Ooh. Just in time I
remember to nip to the loo and snip the string off a tampon.
Shove it up and hope to God it's not the last time I ever see it.
And by seven thirty I'm on the floor. The big new year's eve
night. The Christmas decorations are still up. There's an offer
on champagne. Some wanker's hung a banner with the wrong
year on. There are some other dancers here of course. But the
club itself? Completely dead. Not a single fucking customer.
And the DJ's playing Coldplay. My good intentions start to
waver. I'll just pop to the bar and get a glass of wine. Make it
a large. False economy, isn't it, getting a small. Happy. New.
Year. I think about Leo. About this time last year and – and
then I have to stop thinking and just drink some wine. And
then I feel a bit better. Ah yes. It's not so bad. It's quiet. Yes.
But I have this large glass of white wine which at the moment
is a bit rank but soon will be tasty and soon I'll be relaxed and
then when some customers do come in I'll be ha ha ha I'll
be charming and seductive and and then the waiter pops his
head round and raises his hand and we're watching to see how
many fingers he's going to hold up and suddenly we're on full
alert because it's one. One finger. One customer. A Golden
Egg. This is it. Let's play darts.

So – sorry – yes. The way it works is like this. When men
walk into the club, the first thing we're doing is assessing their
munitary potential. At the bottom of the scale come fifteen
sweaty red faced fat boys in football shirts and feather boas.
Otherwise known as the Stag Party. Now don't get me wrong.
I totally understand why it's important to touch as many girls'
tits as possible before you make a serious commitment to just
one. But why do you need to bring your mates?

The Golden Egg on the other hand, is one rich handsome *young* guy on his own, with a penchant for rescuing sluts a la Pretty Woman, you know. Which never happens so you'll settle for one boring old rich lonely guy who despite the obvious (he's old, he's boring) still seems to believe you find him attractive. Boring old rich lonely guy has money to burn and so long as you strike the right chord, he's yours for the evening. And that means money. Girls come back down from VIP sometimes with massive wads of cash. Not very often. Never happens to me. But you know. If you're really lucky then boring old rich lonely guy might be lonely and stupid enough to keep coming back and then he becomes what they call a *regular*. He's serious about getting dances. He's well into naked girls and stuff. It's all about the naked girls isn't it? Isn't it?

So anyway, that's what I'm thinking. As this guy comes in. Golden Egg. Only thing is, so's everyone else, right? The club is entirely populated by girls waiting to pounce. But no one's allowed to sit down with a customer till he's got his drink right? Club rules. They have to get a drink. So the Egg sits down and straight away there's girls circling him like vultures. Watching his face as he orders…(we're hoping for a big fat wallet and bottles of champagne) and he orders and the waiter goes and there's more circling and then finally here comes the waiter with the drink tray and it's…well okay it's a beer but it's really fucking quiet tonight and the drink goes down on the table and – before you can say happy new year in swoops Destiny there goes Lolita and that's it, I've lost out. As usual. My stage name is Dorothy. I thought it was kind of nineteen forties film noire. But. Yeah.

Two hours and forty five minutes later I'm on the verge of slitting my own throat. My big new year has so far comprised of three large glasses of wine at my own expense and a lengthy chat with a town planner called Matt who's here with his mates on…wait for it…a stag night. Hurrah. Unusual on new year's eve of course, and it's not entirely clear which one of them is supposed to be getting married. Matt says it's his cousin Martin, but I suspect it may just be a rouse to come to a stripclub when

really they should be at home playing party games with their
wives. But it's not all bad. Matt, who it might interest you
to know comes originally from Basingstoke, is an expert on
the roundabouts of Hemel Hempstead, a passion which he's
generously sharing. What Matt is not, however, is showing any
signs whatsoever of having a single fucking dance. Across the
room his mates are working their way steadily through all the
other dancers here. But Matt, apparently, is enjoying our chat
too much. And then he drops his bombshell. He's not sure he's
going to be able to have any dances actually because his wife's
just had a baby and he might feel a bit guilty afterwards. Oh
right. I see. Now it's clear to me at this point that I have one of
two choices. One: smash my wine glass over his shiny balding
head. Or two, make a last ditch attempt to talk the fucker
round. I take a deep breath. Count to three. And go for it. I
lean over, touch his arm. With my other hand I gently stroke
his knee. Listen, I say. Matt. I don't mean to pressure you, but
my mother's back in the homeland and she really needs an
operation on her heart and I'm supposed to be sending money
back at the end of the week. And he's like, the homeland? And
I'm like, yes. And he says, you sound English. And I say, oh
that's very kind of you *[in an accent]* I learn since I was little
child. I love this country. And he says, where are you from?
And I say, uh, Romania? And his eyes light up, you know, cos
now he thinks I'm a dirty eastern European. Maybe he's heard
about the Bulgarian twins who let you finger them for an extra
fiver. Not that they're real twins. But it works in my favour
because at last Matt cracks. All thoughts of his newborn child
now out the window, he finally says yes. Yes? Yes. I get up.
We'll do it here, I say, come on. Quick quick. Open your legs.
Britney comes on. Toxic. Which is good cos I know the words
and I get less nervous if I can sing along while I do the dance.
And yeah. You know. I do it and – it's fine, you know. I mean.
I always think it's a bit weird. It's hardly ever actually sexy. Not
when I do it anyway. Most of the time I just look at their faces
and think, does this really turn you on? Or do you just think
it should? Because it's just my tits. You know? I see em all the
time. But Matt seems to be enjoying himself. And then at the

end, I've managed to get my pants off around my heels which is always a tricky moment, and I say, right you are, time's up, that okay? And he looks down and he's like, what's that?

And I think shit, did I forget to cut the string off my tampon again? But when I look down at my crotch it's just this unfortunate bit of loo roll. Stuck there from when I'd been for a wee. And I'm like, oh it's just a bit of loo roll, and whip it off. He gets this look on his face like maybe he's going to be sick or ask for a refund so I sort of grab my stuff and stumble away, trying to get dressed and get across the other side of the club. Quick as I can in my giant perspex heels, you know.

And that's when I see the Golden Egg. Just sat there on his own. Gleaming in the tacky disco lighting. Matt is kind of making his way up behind me, Egg is beckoning, so I rush forwards and squeeze in beside him.

Since Leo I've – I've had trouble finding other men interesting. Just – maybe because of this place. Or – I don't know. But the Egg, who tells me his name is Darren – he's kind of… there's something about him. He's sort of – fit. And better than that we chat for a few minutes and turns out he's a record producer for some amazing band I've never heard of! This is brilliant! Why is no one else sitting with him? Darren's giving me admiring glances, and I'm thinking, well – you know – maybe he's just not interested in the others. You know? Maybe finally what we have here is a gentleman of some discrimination. A man of taste. And then right there at the table – as one might expect from a head honcho in the *music business* – he offers me a line of coke.

Can I just say I *have* been trying to cut down. I've kind of made this rule to myself that I won't have any until it's time to go on the pole. Johnny doesn't like me to overdo it. But I do in all honesty actually need to be completely cunted before I can do my pole dance. You know? Being sexy is fucking difficult. It's so – I don't know. It's just so *serious*. All this bending and…grinding. Urgh. Which is why on a good night I don't get called to the pole before fantasy hour when

I'm already changed into my fantasy outfit, which in my case
is a nun. Sort of. If nuns wore french knickers and a basque.
But if I'm in my fantasy outfit then I have an excuse to make
my pole dance a bit comedy, which they don't like but I do it
anyway because – well because usually by that point I'm off
my tits. I want Climb Every Mountain as my pole dance song
but Lorna – she's like the club, kind of, boss, madam, kind
of person – she always says no. Makes me dance to Christina
Aguilera which is ridiculous. Would a real nun pole dance to
a song called Dirty? Anyway, so generally I try and save my
coke for that time of the evening, which tends to be much
later when the club is full. But right now, this evening, I'm
a bit shaken up after the whole loo roll crotch incident, plus
this is a freebie, so I accept. And then Darren leans forward
and he says to me can I tell you a secret, and I'm like go on
then. And he says, I've got the biggest cock known to man.
The first of the coke kicks in at the back of my throat. Bang. I
feel this instant amazing sense of total wellbeing and complete
rightness. I'm so fucking okay it's ridiculous. Oh really, I
say. Big cock eh, I say. I glance down. And yeah, you know,
it's – it looks generous enough. I mean, it's hard to see in the
lights, but there's definitely something… *down there.* And I
say God it must be really hard to buy underpants. Do you get
them specially made or? Which is when Lorna appears and
is all like, er, I need to have a word with you? I say I'm sorry
Lorna I'm kind of busy? I'm with the biggest cock known to
man. But she pulls me to one side and tells me a customer has
complained. Matt wants his money back. I'm like oh fuck off
man. For a bit of loo roll? Some people pay extra for that shit.
Who the FUCK does he think he is?

Mmm. She's looking at me funny. Oops. Have I – do I seem
wasted? I don't feel it I feel brilliant but usually when Lorna
talks to me I'm too scared to speak. Shit. Must. Appear.
Normal. I smile. Try and think of something clever to say.
Give her the twenty quid back.

Beat.

What happened then?

Beat.

I remember the countdown. Ten nine eight… Christ. I think me and Darren might have linked arms and sung Auld Lang Syne. I don't really remember I just – I just remember that suddenly it's nearly time to close and all I've done all night is just sit here. Getting twatted. Haven't made any money. Whatsoever. And I'm like, shit. Darren, can you please have a dance? This is supposed to be my big money night and I can't even pay the house commission. And he's like, I don't want a dance. Tell me where you live. And I'm like, ha ha no. You've clearly misunderstood the deal my friend. You pay for dances. Nothing else. And he's like, I don't mean like that I mean – you know. A date. What you doing tonight? I'm like, working. I'm working. And I need some fucking money to get paid. At the very least give me the rest of that coke. You owe me. And he's like, no, fuck off, tell me where you live. And I'm like no way. Fuck you. And he's like, fuck you. Tell me. And – it's too late to call Johnny and it's new year's eve. So I tell him. He says he's going to wait for me outside. After closing.

I have this fantasy for which I think Richard Curtis is entirely responsible. It's the end of the night at work and I haven't made any money again, and I'm miserable and lonely and – this isn't the fantasy – that's actually sort of every night – but in my fantasy I get to the door of the club and outside it's raining and standing there in the rain is Leo. He's waited. All night. Music plays and I run into his arms… and you know what Richard Curtis? You can fuck off. Because the reality is Darren. Waiting in a bit of drizzle. Smoking a joint. And talking – all the way back to my place – about his giant penis.

So anyway, we get back here, do the usual, you know. Nice place you got here. Really? What's that smell? It's chicken. Don't ask. Here's the toilet. Nice. This is the kitchen. Where's the booze? Oh and here's the bedroom.

Suddenly he's like – bam. Throws me on the bed. This big
grin on his face.

Are you ready baby? Yeah look at you, you can't wait.

I'm just lying here, doing as I'm told. Pretty fucked, actually,
and trying to take my pants off. He's wriggling out of his
clothes, jeans flung on the floor, shirt over his head. Standing
there in his boxers and he's all brace yourself baby, reaching
for his crotch. I'm like Jesus, look at it – fuck me that is big –
look at the size of that – packet – of – *weed* he's just pulled out
of his pants and lobbed on the floor and look at that tiny little
willy he's holding. He's beaming, shaking it at me and I'm
staring, trying to work out if this is some kind of joke. I mean,
it's – it's like a baby willy. I kind of want to coo. Who has he
been fucking? Why lie? What a psycho. Fuck it, I need a line.
And I run to the loo and choff the rest of the coke.

Everything seemed a bit better after that. So he's a psycho. So
what? And at least I won't get cystitis.

First thing this morning I'm sleeping and also sort of half
aware of these loud banging noises. I sit up and I'm like,
what the fuck is that and who the fuck are you? And he goes,
I'm Darren. Happy new year. Oh yeah… And that's when
I hear Johnny, outside. Shouting my name. Oh fuck. Shit.
What's he doing here? Suspicious bastard. I told him I was
working. And Darren's like, WHO IS IT? I'm like shut the
FUCK up. Please. That's – it's Johnny. He's – he's not very
nice. He might want to kill us. Darren starts rolling himself a
joint. And I'm like, what are you doing? We have a situation
here. This is hardly the time. He lights up. Au contraire, he
says, he really says that, au contraire. You need to chill out
my friend. Outside, Johnny starts punching the door, and
I'm like shut up Darren. What I need is for you to give me
my money and go home. And he's like what? And I'm like,
my money my money. I need the money from last night. He
takes a toke on his joint. I ain't got no money, he says. I'm
like, what do you mean? You're a record producer. Course
you got money. Nah, he says. I just said that so you'd sit with

me. I just got out of prison three days ago. I was gagging for it. Unbefuckinglievable. I should have known shouldn't I? You know what? Just get out. Go on. Fuck off. He's like, yeah yeah alright. Um…Can you lend me some money? What? I live miles away, he says. I got no cash. No, Darren, I can't. But you're a stripper, he says. You must be loaded. There's a bang like Johnny's going to kick the door down. Shit. Shit. Look! I say! Stroke of genius. Just take my travelcard. Not the door! You'll have to go out the window. You can jump on the roof of that shed.

Beat.

I'm sweating by this point. Like, I really need a line. And I'm intending just to go to the door and act all sleepy and tell Johnny to piss off but then I'm really wired so I end up opening the door and getting some coke off him and then obviously I'm sort of obliged to have sex with him because you know. Well, because he's my boyfriend. And because he just gave me a gram of coke for free. Right? So anyway we do it. Or I should say, he does it. Sometimes with Johnny I like to play this game? It's a bit sick, but it entertains me. It's called play dead. Half way through the act, I just stop breathing. I stop breathing or moving or making any sound and every time I do it I think surely this time he's going to notice but it's amazing because he never does. It's brilliant. Only this time, I'm lying there, my eyes kind of glazed open, my mind wandering, and I suddenly remember the tampon. And I'm trying to remember if I took it out or not because obviously it had no string so I might not necessarily have noticed so I'm thinking maybe it's still up there. And I'm pretty sure you're not supposed to have sex with a tampon in are you? Because of toxic whatsit. And maybe if I was a stronger person, I'd think it was funny but in the moment it's like – Johnny's all grunting and sweating and pushing the fucking thing even further up and maybe into my womb or something and I can't help it I just start – you know – well crying. And eventually he comes, he gets off me and he looks at me and he's like, are you okay?

She laughs.

And I don't know what happens but it's like suddenly –
accidentally – the truth just starts coming out my mouth. Not
about the tampon. But I say No. Actually. I'm not okay. I don't
think I can do this any more. Sorry. I don't want to see you
again. I say it's not at all uncommon for relationships to end at
new year. Apparently. I read that. Ages ago. And he says –

He said

There is a silence. She picks up the notebook.

I believe it's called throwing your toys out of the pram. I won't
– yeah. I don't know what he thought he'd find. But. Anyway.
This was in the bottom of my cupboard. Didn't think I still
had it.

In the end I said if you don't stop I'm going to scream. And
Upstairs will call the police. So he went.

Beat.

Do you ever look at yourself and think, wait a second. No
this – this is wrong. I'm – you know. I'm – this is not me.
I've got things to – someone to be. Astronaut. Celebrity.
Prime minister. What happens to me. Matters. Doesn't it? I'm
important. And then you think about it and you realise…no.
Not really.

She lights a fag. Wipes at her nose. There is some blood.

I just had a funny thought. I could call Leo. Say happy new
year. Yeah. Oh hi Leo. What you been up to? You'll never
guess what's just happened to me… What's he going to do?

*She opens the notebook. Starts to read. The lights change. A screen is
illuminated with a projection:*

1 YEAR EARLIER

5th February

A definition is projected:

Girlfriend

noun.

A person's regular female companion with whom
they have a romantic or sexual relationship.

F is standing at the window.

Fulangst.

Fool. Angst.

Leo's favourite word. It's Norwegian. He likes it because he
says there is no equivalent word in the English language. It
means the guilt that one feels after a night's heavy drinking.
Apparently the Italians have a word for the moist circle
left behind on a table by a hot coffee cup. I don't – can't
remember that one.

Pause.

We met in a car park. Funny isn't it? Where things happen.
On the way to Luton airport. Me and Gemma were picking
him up on the way to our holiday. Gemma from work? My
first proper holiday as a single woman after the end of Mike.
The end of Mike. Sorry. That sounds awful. I don't mean.
I just mean – after Mike. Well. Ended. Anyway, I shouldn't
have gone really. I'm supposed to be saving up to go back to
uni. But it was like fate. They were going together, Gemma,
Leo and Leo's girlfriend Bella. But him and Bella broke up
like – just the week before – so Gemma was like come on! You
should come! I'd not had a holiday since me and Mike went
camping in his mum's back garden. And it was only twenty
quid to change the name on the ticket so…

I've always believed in love at first sight, but I'd never actually
– . Yeah. I just saw him and Gemma said, this is Leo and I said
hello, and I thought you're the most beautiful man I've ever seen.

We get in the car and click, just like that. He's like – he's like
a real grown up. Works in publishing. Dictionaries. He's got
a nice haircut. Plays football on a Sunday. He's really good.
Once had trials for West Brom. Ham? Something like that.

And on the third or fourth night of holiday we go to this
nightclub. Club Ronald it's called. (Ronalde?) And basically
it's just this room in a building but it's got lights and music
and ha look there's a barman in a Hawaiian shirt and there's
literally shit loads of sleazy men all rammed in and grinning at
us going English Girls! Ole!

We push our way through to the bar and order some of those
little apple cocktails. Mmm. Have a few of those, grab a beer
and head for the dance floor. Leo's sitting out but Gemma's
really giving it some you know. Flicking her hair and – this
with her hips and. She keeps coming up to me going *pretend
to be lesbians. They love it.* I'm sort of shuffling, you know. Bit
awkward. Haven't really had enough to drink to really dance
and plus I'm sort of aware of Leo over there. I keep catching his
eye like – I don't know. Just looks. You know. Looking. But then

Hang on – is this? It's Ricky Martin! It is! Now I can do my
Euro-dancing!

She dances. There is fist pumping.

I love this shit this shit's my favourite! These German guys are
giving me strange looks. And Gemma's sort of keeping her
distance but suddenly Leo, who was sort of looking miserable
before, has jumped up and is joining in! And he's hilarious!
And he keeps reaching over and touching my arm and kind of
putting his hand on my waist and – wow. I can't believe this
is happening! This is good. This is bonding! And he goes and
gets more shots. And when the last song comes on, he kind of
steps into me. And we slow dance.

It's the most romantic moment of my life.

And on the walk home we're a bit pissed and he starts telling me about how he's only ever slept with Bella. And I think, oh my God. And Leo is really good looking. He could have any girl he wants. But he really believes in the integrity of sex. Do you think that's weird, he says? And I'm like, no. I think it's amazing. And I remember how someone once told me how if anyone asks you should always say you'd had sex with three people. Because it's like, you've lost your virginity, you've had a fling, and then you've also been in love and learned how to do it properly. But even three in this context sounds a lot so I just say, I mean I myself have only ever slept with two. Do you mind me asking what happened? With – Bella is it? Oh, he says. She just turned into a bit of a nightmare. Went all psycho on me, you know? Oh, I say. Oh no. You don't want that. Anyway yeah. We get back to the apartment and – we go out to the balcony and somehow end up you know. Snogging. Nothing more. Just kissing. The perfect kiss.

And when we get back to England, it's all I talk about.
Leo. Leo. I see signs of him all over.

She's in hospital? Leo's mother is a nurse.

Look, a football. Leo plays football.

You're hungry? Leo's half Hungarian.

Leo has brown eyes. Leo lives in Shepherd's Bush. Leo… is a Sagittarius!

I start looking up our compatibility in magazines. Like I'm thirteen again. Doing those quizzes: Is he your perfect love match? Will you still be together in ten years' time? Answer all the questions so they come out YES.

And of course…we wait to have sex. Like people in love do. Two and a half weeks. So it means something, you know, when we eventually do it. Leo's a bit shy. There's nothing kinky. He doesn't do drugs. He insists we use a condom. Doesn't even want to put it in a bit first you know. And when we *"make love"*, it feels real. It feels like it's supposed to. Sometimes I cry afterwards. Don't know why but it's what you do isn't it? When it really means something.

The perfect couple.

I moved here to be nearer him. It's not ideal. I know. Smells of chicken. From the takeaway downstairs. But it's just round the corner from Leo's so…yeah. He's very spontaneous see? Doesn't do plans. I thought we'd be spending more time together but actually he's always really busy with work and stuff so.

Oh God. I don't know. I mean. What did I expect? Obviously things don't just. You can't just. Can you? What's normal in these situations does anyone know?

Because –

Six months down the line, it's Saturday night for example and we get into bed together – his bed of course, he won't stay at mine – and he's too tired. It's not like – you know – he tries. He doesn't try and is too tired, he just knows already he's too tired and he's got football in the morning and sure enough two seconds later he's snoring. I refer back to my magazines. Take the initiative, they say. Try wearing the football shirt of his favourite team…and nothing else. That sounds good, I think. Now who is it Leo likes? Is it Arsenal or Manchester United but I can't remember all I know is it's someone red and it seems like a potentially disastrous mistake doesn't it? So instead I opt for Ann Summers. Black lace. Nothing fancy. Saturday night comes round. I'm trying it out. I've got this sort of fantasy that we'll just get down to it in the living room and he'll slowly undress me and the sight of black lace will send him wild with desire but in fact Match of the Day is on and when it ends he just gets up, turns off the telly and says you coming to bed?

Yeah.

Follow him in. He goes in the bathroom and while he's gone I take this opportunity to get undressed and sort of – you know – arrange myself on the bed. He's ages. I keep getting stiff. He must be doing a poo. Come on. Are you okay in there? Yeah, he says. Just reading. Oh. Anyway, finally I hear the chain flush and I try and limber up a bit. Tousle my hair. And

Leo comes to the doorway. He looks at me. Frowns. He says: What are you doing?

Beat.

It's – I don't know what to say. Isn't it obvious? I'm seducing you, I want to say. Aren't I? But instead I say: I got it for you, I thought you'd like it. He says: I've got a headache. Gets into bed. Still wearing his socks.

You've got a headache??

What?

Isn't that my line?

Oh not this again.

No– just-

I'm just tired, he says. Do you think going on at me's going to put me in the mood?

Don't you love me anymore?

Fuck's sake, he says. Don't go psycho. Course I love you. You know I love you. He kisses me on the nose. I'm just tired.

Turns out the light.

But men are obsessed with sex. Aren't they? They're supposed to think about it every six seconds. What's wrong with me?

And I keep thinking about Mike. Because of course it was a fuck up, you know? I mean, he'd tell you that himself. If he – do they have phones in rehab? I don't know. It's just Mike always said true love is the yin and the yang. Two halves of a whole. Two – you know. Become *one*. But with Leo I just keep getting this feeling that what he really wants is for me to go back to who I was before I was his girlfriend. But that feels impossible to achieve because actually – This is who I am. I'm – I'm messy. I get cross. I'm – neurotic. Sometimes I wake him up and make him check outside for murderers and sometimes I'm really fucking horrible and mean. I moan about my job all the time. I fart. It smells. I'm – I don' t know. I'm not perfect. And he – he still is. I still think he is.

Beat.

I've built my whole future round him, you know? I haven't told Leo because he doesn't like to talk about the future, but he's got such a great surname and it really goes with mine and I just think we'd have the most beautiful children and this is it. This is the one I've been waiting for.

And then yesterday.

On the most romantic day of the year…

I wait in for the post. All day at work I'm expecting flowers. And eventually I crack. Call him up. Oh shit. He says. No way. Is it today? I'm going out with the boys. Anyway, he says, I thought you said you weren't into all that Valentine's day shit.

I know what I'm supposed to say. No worries, I'm supposed to say. Let's take a rain check. I'm cool. I'm busy. And I nearly manage, I do but instead there's just this:

Loaded silence.

I mean. Of course Valentine's is shit but still. He should WANT to do something. Shouldn't he? He should be overwhelmed with romantic ideas to surprise me with. Roses in the bathtub. Or whatever. A ring in a glass of champagne. Not going out to play pool with *Jamo*. This is fucking outrageous. He doesn't *love* me. This isn't *love*. This isn't what people in *love* do. Fine, I say, as though fine as a word actually means the exact opposite of the word fine. As though fine means bastard. Or Hitler. And I slam down the phone. I don't need this shit. I go round to Gemma's desk. Let's go out, I say. Girlie night. We haven't been out together for ages. So we fuck off down the pub. Bottle of white. Then another. Then a round of tequilas. Then another. Fuck men, I'm shouting. CALL THAT LOVE? And somehow –

Beat.

– at some point – after many – many tequilas – I find myself pouring out my troubles to this red faced banker. And the way he's looking at me I just – I feel – I just want to feel wanted.

And this morning I wake up and reach out, thinking it's Leo. And when I turn over it's – it's not. And I feel –

Fulangst.

Go downstairs to get a glass of water. Past the front door and on the doormat is a red envelope.

To my Valentine, it says. Let's do tonight instead.

Pause.

And I wish it was enough. But is it? Because I think I finally get it, you know? There is no salvation. No one is coming to save me. This is it.

Lights change.

A screen is illuminated with a projection:

2 YEARS EARLIER

25th December

A definition is projected:

Victim

noun.

1. a person harmed, injured or killed as a result of a crime, accident or other event or action.

2. a person who is tricked or duped.

3. a person who has come to feel helpless and passive in the face of misfortune or illtreatment.

F is sitting on the bed wearing a cumbersome beige fleece several sizes too large.

Mike says life is a journey. And on that journey we will make many discoveries. We will suffer pain and also experience great joy. Without pain, he says, joy would not exist. And without love, there would be no fear. Which makes me think, you know. Without the secret there would have been no Ian. And without Ian there would have been no vow. And without the vow – well.

I mean. I'm glad – I'm glad the vow is broken. I'm glad because it's brought things into the open and one little thing doesn't matter does it? It's just a detail. Not the end of the world. Global warming is the end of the world. The sea levels. Sometimes you have to look at the bigger picture and the bigger picture is that Mike is going to save the planet. And I'm going to help. And I shall do it all wearing this miraculous new fleece, what do you think? It's my present from Mike! I should have said. Yeah I really like it. It's supposed to withstand temperatures as low as you get in the Arctic apparently. You have to wear it under a cagoule which I don't have but it's okay because Mike's got a spare. Then its insulatory potential will be massive. So. It's brilliant. I wasn't expecting anything material to be honest. Mike says Christmas has massacred the pagan tradition. Kill a tree? he said. For decoration? Which I felt a bit sad about but he's right I think. It's not like you need a tree is it? It's not like you need anything. You don't need high heels, Mike says. You look better in trainers. You, he says, would look good in a sack.

Beat.

She looks down at the fleece.

But anyway, yesterday. Mike was on campus see? And he rang and said he'd be late home. Only I'd run out of my special sleeping pills and I panicked in case we couldn't get them before Pothead Dave went home for Christmas. So I told Mike I'd go and pick them up. Mike said, no babe. That's okay. It's dark. You don't know what you're doing. But I was like, no. It'll be fine. Don't worry.

Which I wished I'd never said because fuck me. I set off and the way to Pothead Dave's is literally riddled with dangers. Busy roads. Men walking dogs. Cracks in the pavement. And I have to say to myself, life is a journey but even so by the time I get there I feel like I'm having a nervous breakdown. I mean. Well. And I knock on the door and here comes Mike's best friend. Little Mike. Come in dude, he says. Long time no see. I go into in the hallway. Bit nervous, you know, lest there be a jam session underway but thankfully it's all quiet. Ooh. I might even get a cup of tea. Not real tea. Obviously. You don't drink Tetley if you've had a gap year. Little Mike, for example, has drunk nothing but hot water since his year in Tibet. Teaching English to a Llama. Not the Dalai. One of the younger incarnations. Oh that reminds me. Must take off my shoes.

She bows with hands pressed together.

Sign of respect.

And it occurs to me that the last time I came here was just before I told Mike the secret. Feels like a different – life.

Hello?

I wander to the living room.

Easy. (It's Pothead Dave.) What's up?

Hi Dave. How you doing? One thing about Mike's friends.
None of them are ever just okay. Or fine. They're always:
Amazing yeah. I saw a fox. In the garden. It was totally wild
man. I'm not sure what to say. I glance nervously at Pothead
Dave's guitar, the one he got in Vietnam. And a bongo drum,
that's new. And oh wait look – against the far wall someone's
built a pyramid from empty cans of Tennent's. Haven't seen
you in ages, Dave's saying. Mike says you're sick. Does he?
Oh. I – I just need that stuff you said – I've got your money –
Arrgh! *Dave makes the sign of the cross.* Hates money of course.
Money is like totally responsible for loads of evil and Take a
pew dude, he says. Stay and chat. Oh I can't, I say. I'm kind
of in a hurry. Mike said you said you'd have them ready. Dave
frowns. I'm upsetting his zen. Shit. I try to smile. Sorry, I say. I
just – I really need them. Sure dude, he says. Gets up and goes
to a drawer. This should keep you going, he says. Gives me a
bag of pills. Thanks, I say. I've got to go. Sorry. See you Dave.
Bye Little Mike! I go back out into the hall. Shoes, check.
Medicine, check. Ready to go. Check. Life is a journey.

Beat.

Check.

Oh God. I can't. I can't go out there. Nothing on earth will
make me. I'm on the verge of giving up and going back in
when I hear from the living room the unmistakeable sound
of Pothead Dave's guitar plucking out the beginning strains of
Stairway to Heaven and yep – that does the trick! I slam open
the front door and hit the ground running.

Mike says one of the things that drew me to him was my air
of mystery. You were very mysterious, he says. With your
vow and your secrets. When I first told him about the vow
I thought I'd put him off but in fact he almost seemed more
keen. You've given up sex, he said. Forever? Oh yes, I said.

Forever. Cool, he said. You're like a monk. But then, after
a bit, he starts asking me. Why? he says. Did something
happen? I'm like, no no. It's nothing. Just something I did.
Nothing bad. And then a few weeks later he says, you know. If
I'm to be supportive of this vow, I think I should at least know
why. And by this time, I – well. I don't know. I – I care about
him. I suppose – I trust him.

So I tell him. The secret. About what I did. And: That's
terrible, he says. I know. No, he says. I don't mean that. I
mean that wasn't your fault. I'm smiling. What's he saying?
I'm like, what do you mean? It sounds to me like you were
the victim, he says. And certainly, it's no reason not to have
sex again. Which is when I think about Ian. I can't not tell
him that bit of the story. Can I? But I like the way he's looking
at me. All sad and – sympathetic. I don't want that look to
change to something else. So I just nod and he holds my hand.
Strokes it a bit with his thumb. We ought to try, Mike says.
Some time. But listen. We take it at your own pace. When
you're good and ready. When I'm good and ready. I get
back here. Just after five. Mike's not back. And I saw a raven
on Cobbold Street so maybe he's dead. Maybe he's been
murdered. Oh god. I'm freaking out. I need to take a pill. Get
out my new stash. Ooh. Look at them all. Lots of pills. I pop
one in my mouth. I'm expecting The blissful falling of a heavy
blanket. Oblivion.

But by the time Mike gets back... I've put his Eric Clapton
cd on. It's the most beautiful thing I've ever heard. I'm crying
at its sheer incredible beauty. I'm laughing too because I'm
extraordinarily happy. I dance and I'm so – fucking – free. I'm
an amazing human being. An animal. A creature of God. I'm
filled with the shiny sunlight of love and peace and suddenly
I know what Mike's talking about it's like – this is zen this is
karma this is the joy the pain the love the love I get it I get it
and here he is – he's back! Oh my god this is unbelievable!

Are you okay, he says?

I'm fucking amazing.

Did you take something? A temazepan, I say. But I'm not sleepy! A temazapan? he says. Just one, I say. Come on, I say. Forget about the past. Forget that shit. Live for the present, I say. Let's break the vow.

Beat.

This morning he says how do you feel? I'm like fine, I mean – amazing. Bit odd. I don't know. Like – like I've just lost my virginity. He smiles. You broke the vow, he says. For me.

She laughs.

Yeah.

He frowns. Looks down. There's a hair, one of his, on the pillow. He starts flicking it with his finger. You okay? I say. There's something I need to tell you, he says. Oh. Okay. Many discoveries, yeah? On the journey of life. I'm sorry, he says. I – I should have told you – I – before – I just – I don't know why I didn't. It's okay, I say. Go on. And he tells me the story of his ex-girlfriend. Clementine. If you can believe that. He might have said they were engaged, I can't remember. Because then he says how turns out she'd been sleeping around behind his back. And he only found out because one day he started to feel ill. Like he had flu. Then his dick felt sore.

He starts crying. He's got *herpes*?

Beat.

And for a second I don't – I don't know what to say. I mean – I feel awful because this is my chance isn't it – to – to be supportive but – all I keep thinking is – and I have to say it –

But we didn't use a condom.

Oh don't worry, he says. I don't have an attack at the moment. So it's really unlikely you've caught it. And of course I'll take you to the clinic, he says. To – you know. Have the tests.

He takes my hand.

You – you trusted me, he says. With your secret. So I thought – I don't know. I just – I've never told anyone that before.

And it's like – I don't know but now I'm crying too and I just put my arms around him and he does and we hold on to each other and then suddenly he starts laughing. He's laughing and crying at the same time and I'm like what?

What?

And he says shit man, he says. Fuck man. He says. Look at us:

She laughs.

We're so fucked up.

Lights change.

A screen is illuminated with a projection:

1 YEAR EARLIER
2nd January

A definition is projected:

Bitch

noun.

1.   A female canine animal, especially a dog. Offensive:

2.   A lewd woman.

3.   A man considered to be weak or contemptible

A new definition is added:

verb. trad.

To botch; bungle. Often used with *up*.

F is pacing around her bedroom.

The worst thing is, he said he'd dump her. Asked if I'd be his girlfriend. And I had to say to him, no Ian. This is what is known as a one night stand. People go out. They get fucked. They have sex. Mostly with total strangers. They don't even remember what happened. How they got there. I do this sort of shit all the fucking time now.

He goes really?

I'm like

She makes a noise. Something akin to an uh-huh but one without conviction.

He says, but we didn't use a condom.

I'm like I took the morning after pill this morning. Don't worry about it.

This morning, he says. Why?

I'm like, why? Why? Mind your own fucking business. Why. Why do you think? Anyway I'll see you later, I've got to go. Don't you want to stay? he says. And I don't really mean to but I laugh. And I look at him. And I say No.

Anyway I get back and I'm thinking, this is good. You know? Not good. It's obviously it's disastrous. I mean Sheryl is a geordie. If she finds out, she will kill me. But it's done now, that's the main thing. Shut the fuck up! No one cares about your stupid – just – fuck's sake! Ian's the one who should feel guilty. It's not like she's my friend. I mean. I know her. Yeah. She's in my seminar group. She helps me out. Sometimes. Quite a lot. She's very clever actually. But what? Yeah not that clever because I just fucked her boyfriend. Ha. So? He'd been flirting with me for months. And you know, I needed to fuck someone so I fucked him. Okay? She was in fucking Newcastle. It's not my fault if she hasn't bothered to come back for new year's. Or – you know. Whatever. She's with her sick mother. But I didn't know that. He's the one that should feel guilty.

She covers her eyes. There is a long pause.

The point is, what I'm trying to say is, there's nothing I can do. You can't turn back the clock. You can't remember. You can't remember. Just move on. Just. Put it all behind you. And move on.

Lights change.

Music.

A screen is illuminated with a projection:

22 HOURS EARLIER

1st January

A definition is projected. It stays on the screen throughout the scene, and the music plays throughout.

Object

(bj kt,-j kt) noun.

1. Something perceptible by one or more of the senses, especially by vision or touch; a material thing.

2. A focus of attention, feeling, thought, or action: *an object of* contempt.

3. The purpose, aim, or goal of a specific action or effort: *the object* of the game.

4. *Grammar* a. A noun, pronoun, or noun phrase that receives or is affected by the action of a verb within a sentence. b. A noun or substantive governed by a preposition.

5. *Philosophy* Something intelligible or perceptible by the mind.

F is on a bed. There is a man sleeping in the bed beside her. He is under the covers, sleeping. She is fully dressed, but her trousers are undone.

Another projection is illuminated:

Object

(b-j kt) verb. intr.

1. To present a dissenting or opposing argument; raise an objection.

F wakes up, sits bolt upright. Stares. Turns slowly and looks at the man. Questions are projected slowly at first, onto the screen. They can rotate, perhaps. Over and over. If there is time for that.

Where am I? It's the man who bought you the drink. The old man who bought me the drink. Whore

Do I remember midnight? I don't remember midnight. That's my shoe. Where's my bag? What street is that?

Blackout.

The screen is illuminated with a projection:

1 1/2 YEARS EARLIER

19th August

A definition is projected:

Virgin

noun.

1. a person who has never had sexual intercourse.
2. person who is naïve, innocent or inexperienced
in a particular context

Another definition is added:

adjective.

1. being related to, or appropriate for a virgin
2. not yet used, exploited or processed.

My first time? Yeah. Oh god. Well, um if I can remember that
far back I think it was in a caravan in Wales. I would have
been – thirteen? He was a – a local fisherlad, name of Daffyd
Daffo.

Uh, the second time was a one night stand – but like – a really
passionate one that really meant something. But yeah he was
married. So we both sort of agreed you know. Not to – again.
So. Kieran, his name was. Kieran O' Connor.

And the third time I was about fifteen I think and I was
spending the summer on an Israeli kibbutz. He was the group
leader. Moroccan Jim. That one's my favourite. Moroccan Jim
had an eye-patch and seven wives. We really loved each other
but his brother kept trying to sell me for a camel so I had to
come back to England to get away.

Well. I mean – what are you supposed to say? When I think
about my friends, and I think about how – all what they've done
and I've just basically sat in my room my whole life listening to
Kate Bush and pretending to be medieval. Till Steve.

Course I haven't been to an Israeli kibbutz. I've never been to Wales. I'd never even kissed anyone till I was seventeen and I met Steve. I had to do something. There was no way I was going to start university a virgin. Claire says it's our big chance to reinvent ourselves as something better than we've been at school. Which for me means I just want to be able to talk about – sex – my sex-life – have a sex-life – normally like a normal person.

Like, yesterday before we picked up our envelopes I said to her you know, how it had been about six months now and that I was thinking of maybe doing it with Steve. And she said he's not the first is he? And I said, no course not. God. He'd be the – Daffyd, Kieran, (Jim) – fourth. Why what about you? And she said, fuck I don't know. You lose count don't you. Maybe twenty? I was like – eh – really? I'm not a slag, she said. No course, I said, thinking TWENTY? What a slag. Not that I believe in slags. I don't – I mean. I think women should be able to – and it's fine – I'm not a prude. I'm not frigid. That's not – I mean – I don't know. What am I talking about?

So last night, right, my mum's away on a course in High Wycombe and I've drunk three cans of lager and I say to Steve, Steve have you got any condoms? He says I've got one. In my wallet. Why? And I say, because we might need one. He says you don't mean for water bombs do you? I say no.

And he says, oh. Wow. Are you sure?

Yes.

Can we do it in your mum's bed?

No.

The only question I have really is about logistics. I mean. Not logistics what do I mean? Semantics? Something. What I mean is, and I mean, I know you won't know the answer to this but

What happened was

It sort of went – hard – you know how it does – and then it went in – and then it went

I mean there was blood on the toilet paper when I went to the loo so technically – I mean – I'm technically not a virgin any more am I. Am I? We were both sort of a bit wankered. Can't remember whole bits of last night. But waking up was really nice. I mean. It's – it's – it's not what I'm here for. That's a stupid thing to say. But it's just, one of the things that people do that I want to do to and that I've never done. I want to be in love. I want to be loved and have romance and to get that, to have that, it has to start being real. You know? Steve really likes me. And no one else has ever (offered). I have to – not lower my expectations – just – change them. Get with the times. I spent so much time waiting and dreaming and hoping and now I just kind of realise you just need to drink a few pints and then you can do anything.

Steve's gone to the shop. He's says he's going to buy a better condom so we can do it again. Better.

So. Yeah. Results! Two A's and a B and not a virgin.

Moroccan Jim.

I don't know. It's like – I don't know – I've become – like after all these years of being a girl. I've – I'm finally a woman.

FADE.

LIGHTS.

A screen is illuminated with a projection. The quality is that of a silent movie dialogue:

TODAY.

A projection is added:

Right now.

F reads from the notebook.

And so it was that the Lady Ermeldadrew perished of the great
plague. And true to his word, the great Duke Lionarm came
back for the peasant Isabella. He built her a great castle and
lavished on her all the riches of his kingdom. And though for
many days he had to leave her behind to go and fight great
wars, she was always there, waiting for his return. Patient and
true and good. As faithful as a beautiful hound, Isabella loved
the Duke with all her heart. And they lived, as she had always
known they would:

happily…

ever…

Beat.

I mean

Actually.

Hang on a sec. I just need a –

She retrieves a pen from somewhere. Begins to write.

One day the peasant Isabella got bored of waiting around.
She got bored of mopping the Duke's brow when he came
back from war. She said: This is really amazingly dull. Why
did I ever want this? I can't remember. And so it was that the
peasant Isabella ran off and lived in a cottage by herself and
ate many bags of doritos. She watched many episodes of *Star
Trek* and stopped shaving her armpits. Forever. And she did
other stuff too. Important things of great meaning to the world
and to history. First she became an astronaut and eventually,
at a grand old age when she was wrinkly but still deemed

attractive and worthwhile, she was elected prime minister. But did she marry? Did she have children? Well let me think. Did Winston Churchill? Did Neil Armstrong? Um. I don't know. Can't remember. Does it matter? She might have done. She might not:

And no one…

was bothered…

either way.

Blackout.

The End.

By the same author

Meek
9781786826152

Fred's Diner
9781849434867

WWW.OBERONBOOKS.COM

Milton Keynes UK
Ingram Content Group UK Ltd.
UKHW022358301124
451853UK00011B/290